tree house

Builders

Written + illustrated
By
Weston daniel vasquez

credo
house publishers

Published in the United States of America by Credo House Publishers,
a division of Credo Communications LLC, Grand Rapids, Michigan
credohousepublishers.com

ISBN: 978-1-62586-202-0

Cover and interior layout by Sharon VanLoozenoord

Printed in the United States of America
First edition

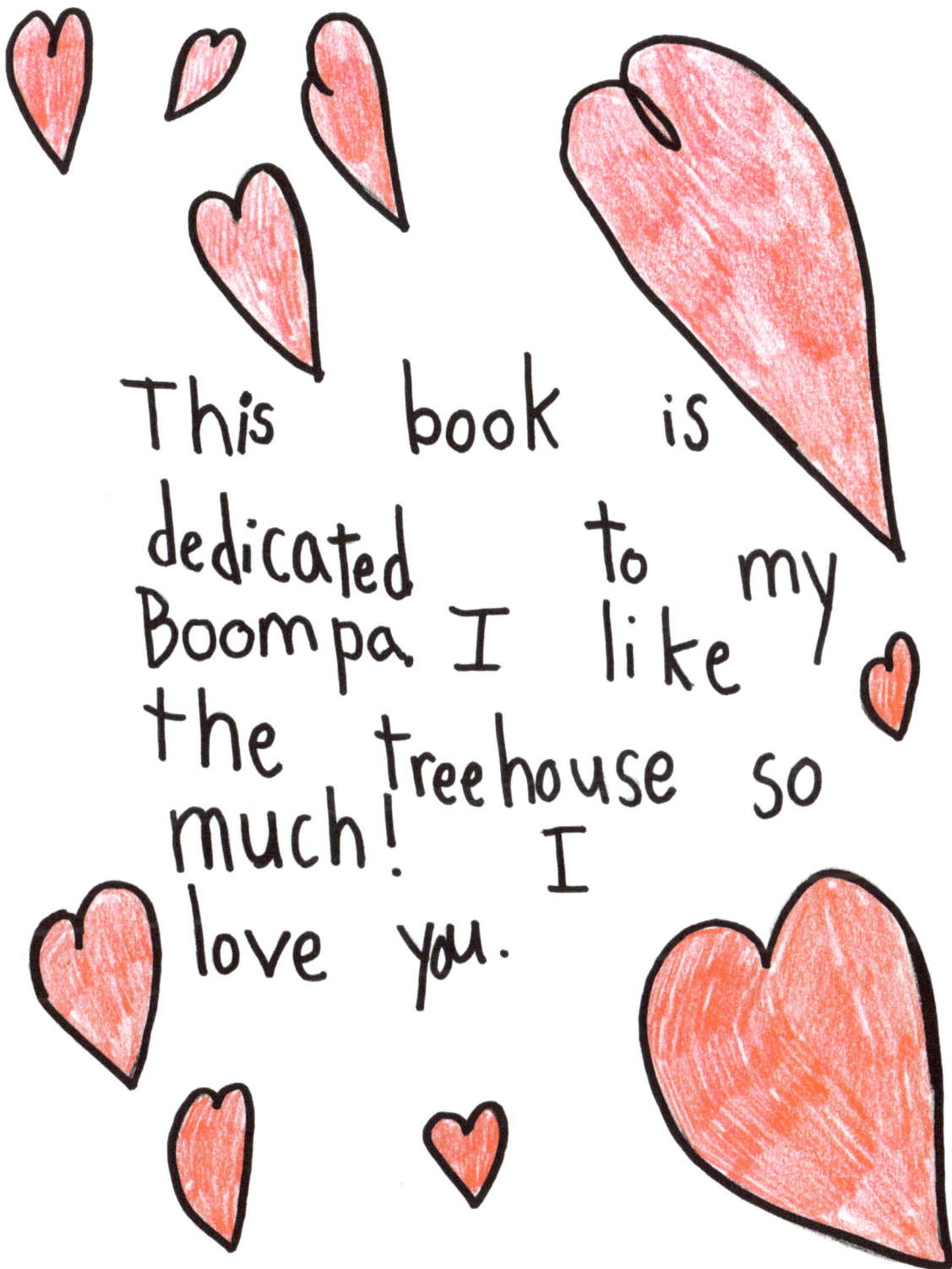

This book is dedicated to my Boompa I like the treehouse so much! I love you.

This is a story about a boy and his Boompa working together to build a

Treehouse

First,
Find a
Boompa
Who
can
Build
STUFF

For your birthday ask Your
Boompa if he will build you
a treehouse.

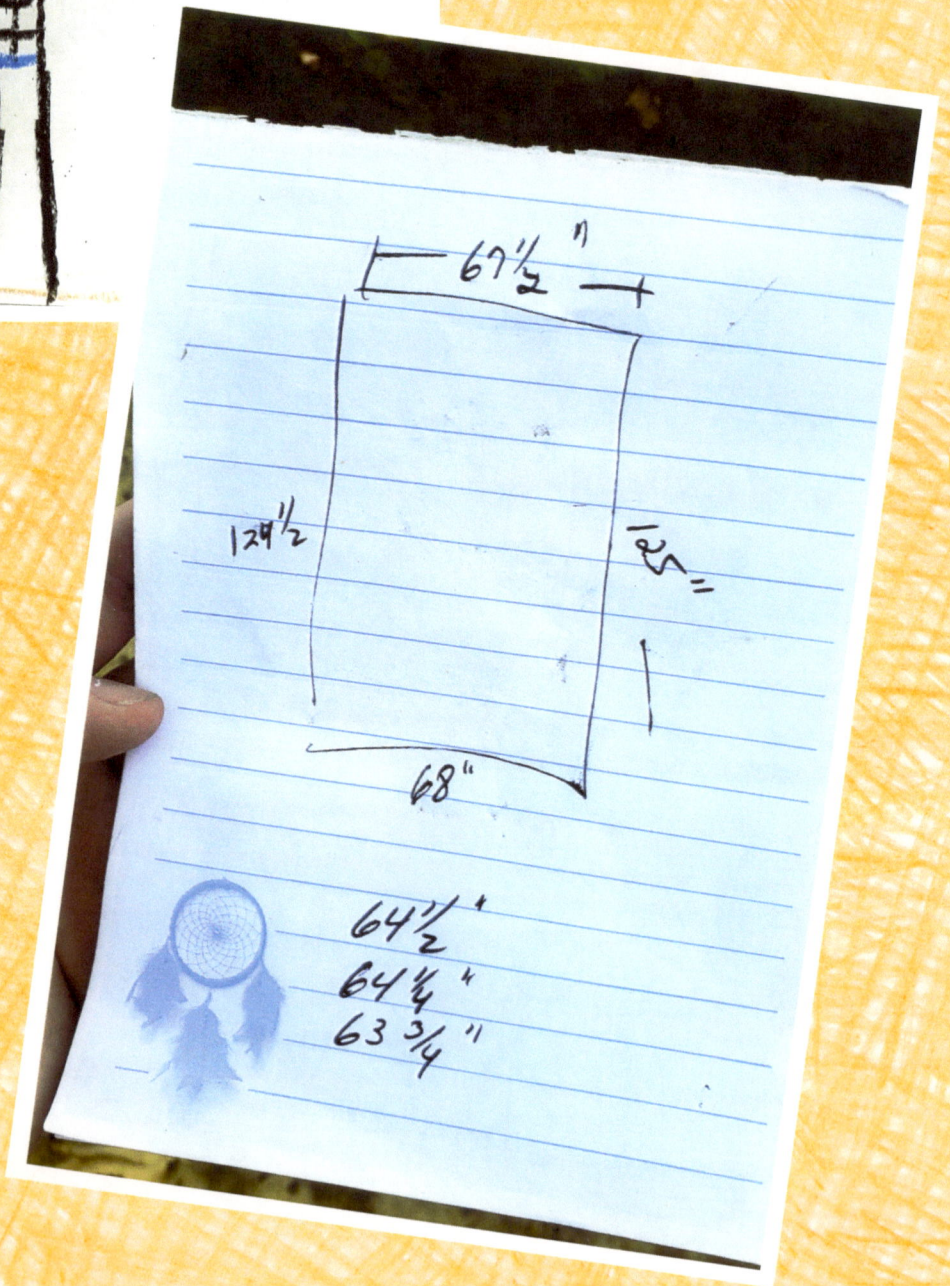

Next, go to the store and get 4 tall wood posts.

next,
cement
the post
into the
ground.

Wait a few days for it to settle...

Make a floor and for stairs the tree house.

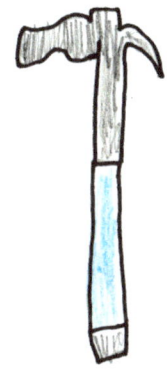

Wait all winter because Boompa's don't work in The cold.

When it gets
warmer have
your Boompa
bring over a saw
and more wood.
measure twice,
cut once!

Yo isa una
es.

Decide or
for your
Next,

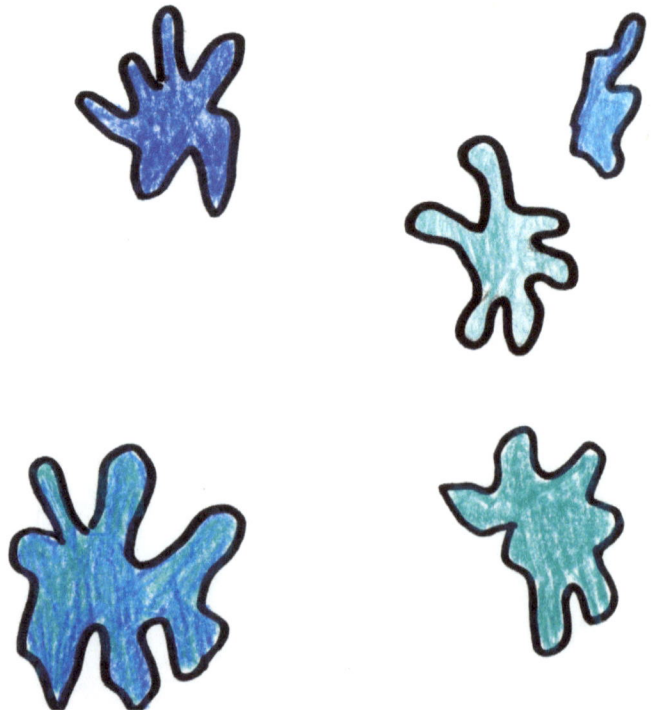

a color
Tree house.
paint it!

Having a tree house is really good but having a Boompa to spend time with is even

better!

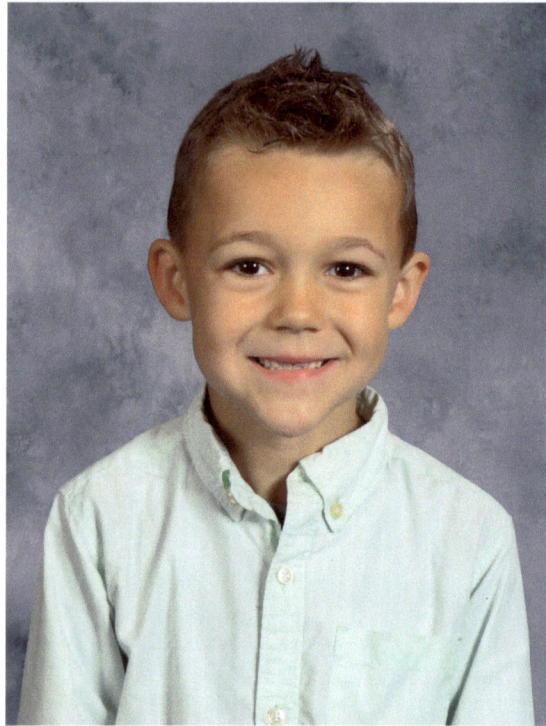

About the Author

weston is 6 years old and in Kindergarten. He attends school in Grandville, Michigan. weston loves to be outside and do arts and crafts.

www.ingramcontent.com/pod-product-compliance
Lightning Source LLC
LaVergne TN
LVHW072105070426

835508LV00003B/281